# Remaking the Earth

"I saw that the sacred hoop of my people was one of many hoops that made one circle, wide as daylight and as starlight, and in the center grew one mighty flowering tree to shelter all the children of one mother and one father. And I saw it was holy."

—Nicholas Black Elk (Lakota)

# Remaking the Earth

*A Creation Story
from the Great Plains of North America
written and illustrated by* **Paul Goble**

Orchard Books  New York

Library of Congress Cataloging-in-Publication Data. Goble, Paul. Remaking the earth : a creation story from the Great Plains of North America / written and illustrated by Paul Goble. p.    cm. Includes bibliographical references. Summary: In the Algonquin ''Earth Diver'' creation myth, the water birds and animals left behind when the old world was flooded dive for mud so that the Creator can make dry land again.
ISBN 0-531-09524-X.—ISBN 0-531-08874-X (lib. bdg.)
1. Algonquin Indians—Folklore. 2. Creation—Great Plains—Mythology. 3. Legends—Great Plains. [1. Algonquin Indians—Folklore. 2. Indians of North America—Great Plains—Folklore. 3. Folklore—Great Plains. 4. Creation—Folklore.] I. Title.
E99.A349.G63 1996        398.2'089973—dc20        [E]        96-4243

References
*These are listed with their original publication details, but most are available in recent editions:* Joseph Epes Brown, **The Spiritual Legacy of the American Indian,** Crossroad Publishing Company, New York, 1982 (ch. 6); **The Sacred Pipe—Black Elk's Account of the Seven Rites of the Oglala Sioux,** University of Oklahoma Press, Norman, 1953 (9); **Animals of the Soul—Sacred Animals of the Oglala Sioux,** Element Inc., Rockport, 1992; Ella Elizabeth Clark, **Indian Legends from the Northern Rockies,** University of Oklahoma Press, Norman, 1966 (220ff. & 235ff.); W. P. Clark, **The Indian Sign Language,** L. R. Hamersly & Co., Philadelphia, 1885 (42ff.); Natalie Curtis, **The Indians' Book,** Harper & Bros., New York, 1907; James O. Dorsey, **A Study of Siouan Indian Cults,** 11th. Annual Report of the Bureau of American Ethnology, Smithsonian Institution, Washington, D.C., 1894; George Amos Dorsey and Alfred L. Kroeber, **Traditions of the Arapaho,** Field Museum of Natural History, Anthropological Series, Vol. V, Chicago, 1903 (1ff.); Richard Erdoes, **The Sound of Flutes and Other Indian Legends,** Pantheon Books, New York, 1976 (126); George Bird Grinnell, **By Cheyenne Campfires,** Yale University Press, New Haven, 1926 (242); **Blackfoot Lodge Tales—The Story of a Prairie People,** Charles Scribner's Sons, New York, 1892 (272); **Some Early Cheyenne Tales,** Journal of American Folk-lore, Vol. XX, No. LXXVIII, 1907 (170); **The Cheyenne Indians—Their History and Ways of Life,** Yale University Press, New Haven, 1923 (90, 91, 337ff.); Alice Marriott and Carol K. Rachlin, **American Indian Mythology,** Thomas Y. Crowell Company, New York, 1968 (21); **Plains Indian Mythology,** Thomas Y. Crowell Company, New York, 1975 (26); James Mooney, **The Ghost-Dance Religion, and the Sioux Outbreak of 1890,** Fourteenth Annual Report of the Bureau of American Ethnology, Part 2, Washington, D.C., 1896 (207); John G. Neihardt, **Black Elk Speaks—Being the Life Story of a Holy Man of the Oglala Sioux,** William Morrow and Co., New York, 1932 (34, for the quotation on the title spread); Marco Pallis, **The Way and the Mountain,** Peter Owen, London, 1960 (ch. 2); Peter J. Powell, **''Beauty for New Life,''** in **The Native American Heritage, A Survey of North American Indian Art,** University of Nebraska Press, Lincoln, 1977 (44); Lewes Spence, **Myths of the North American Indians,** G. G. Harrap, London, 1914 (107ff.); Stith Thompson, **Tales of the North American Indians,** Indiana University Press, Bloomington, 1929 (Notes 29, 30, 31, 57); Clark Wissler and D. C. Duvall, **Mythology of the Blackfoot Indians,** Anthropological Papers of the American Museum of Natural History, New York, 1909 (7, 8, & 19).

*for*
*Anthony and Janne Goble*
*John and Lorraine Wood*
*Geoffrey and Jean Curtis*
*Peter and Pat Hurford*
*Sion and Mary Jones*
*Hélène Wellington*
*Susan Blakiston*
*Peter Metcalfe*
*Beryl Payne*
*Edna Goble*

## AUTHOR'S NOTE

For Indian peoples, Creation is going on all the time. There have been worlds before this one, and there will be others in the future. There is a sense of experimentation and humor, and of the Creator needing the help of already-created beings. Sometimes told over a ritual four-day period, Creation stories include the beginnings of almost everything: how people were first given fire and bows and arrows, and how they learned to hunt. There are stories about how familiar hills and valleys were formed, how birds and animals came to look as they do today, the gift of horses, and even the coming of white people.

Missionaries of every Christian denomination were among the very first white people to make contact with the tribes. They ridiculed the traditional beliefs, with the result that Creation stories, which were first recorded about 1900, show some influence of the Book of Genesis, which I have tried to filter out. Since that time the destructive influences have been more subtle, and most Native American myths have not ''translated'' well into twentieth-century thought. What remains are only fragments of the old stories. They are the closest we can get to the myths as they were told during ''Buffalo Days.''

I have taken ideas from these old stories and woven them into the Algonquin ''Earth Diver'' Creation myth, in which the water birds and animals, left behind when the old world was flooded, dive for mud so that the Creator can make dry land again. Here the elements are Plains Algonquin, mostly Cheyenne, although many are also found in the stories of the Blackfoot and Arapaho peoples. The ideas about the end of this world bring the story into our own times and then back, to complete the cycle of Creation. Although these final ideas are not Algonquin, together with the quotation on page two, I think they speak for all traditions today. When I first thought of doing this book twelve years ago, I was encouraged by my lifelong teacher, Marco Pallis, to write it as a ''spiritual essay.'' I do not think I have succeeded in this, but I hope, in this brief format, to have retained something of the spirit of the old stories, and I hope that this will be an introduction, encouraging people to explore the rich diversity of the old myths. Some of these are listed in the references.

I have not illustrated Earth Maker as a person because there is no precedent for this in Native American painting. Perhaps we see the Creator, the Great Spirit, God, when we see with our hearts and minds all the things which he has made?

*Paul Goble*
*Lincoln, Nebraska, 1996*

Long ago there was another world, like our own, but at one time the mountains crumbled, the earth cracked open, water gushed out and covered up everything. Nothing of the old world could be seen above the water: not the tops of the mighty cottonwood trees, not even the highest hilltop. It was a time of darkness, of dread and calamity.

The only living things were the fishes in the depths and the ducks and animals who lived in the water. The air was filled with the clamor of their wailings. Everyone huddled together, swimming hither and thither, crying out in the voice each knew: "Earth Maker!* Earth Maker! We want to live! Do not leave us to die! Give us back the land so we can rest and have a place to lay our eggs!"

*"Earth Maker" is another name for the Creator, the Great Spirit, or God.

Earth Maker heard their cries. ''I will help you,'' he told them, and at his words everyone took heart. ''One of you must help me: I need mud to make land. Who will dive down and bring me some?''

''I will,'' Mallard Duck called out. He stretched his neck down into the water, but he could not even see the bottom.*

Earth Maker asked again: ''Who will bring me some mud?''

Beaver smacked her broad tail on the water. ''I will bring you some mud.'' She dived, and after her, Grebe, but neither of them could reach the bottom.

*Today Mallards are still searching!

Earth Maker asked a fourth time: "Is there anyone who can bring me mud?"

"I will try," said the little black Coot, and she dived out of sight. When she did not reappear, everyone thought she had been swept away. Suddenly Earth Maker reached down into the water and brought out the almost lifeless Coot. She was too tired to speak, but there was mud on her beak!*

* Coots proudly wear dried mud on their beaks
   as a mark of honor.

Earth Maker scraped the mud from the little Coot's beak. "One of you must carry this mud," he said, and everyone wanted to carry it. He looked lovingly at all of them, and he chose Turtle. "Grandmother Turtle, your back is strong, and you are careful. *You* will carry this mud. You will always be my joy! Your clothes will be glorious, and all life will come from inside you."*

Earth Maker worked the wet mud in his fingers until it was dry. He sprinkled it on Turtle's shell, and with his power the mud grew and grew, until it completely covered Grandmother Turtle and became the earth on which we walk.**

"Now you can rest," he told the birds and animals, and immediately they left the water, giving thanks to Earth Maker.

\* Turtles walk slowly because they remember Grandmother Turtle,
who carries our world on her back. When she moves, there are earthquakes.
\*\* North America is called "Turtle Island."

With the power of his imagination, Earth Maker piled up the mountains and smoothed the plains, letting in just enough water to fill the rivers and lakes and prairie ponds. He splashed paints on the ground, red here and yellow and white there.

The mountains he covered with rocks, pine trees, and snow, and the plains with grasses and flowers. To everything he gave its own scent, and he composed the music of falling rain and wind in the pine trees.

He made roots and berries grow in their rightful places, turnips, buffalo berries, chokecherries, rosehips, and plums. He made each different: some sweet, some sour, so that he did not get tired of any of them.

He scattered cedar trees on the hillsides, and along the streams he planted great cottonwood trees, to enjoy their shade and the sound of their leaves during the heat of the day.

Earth Maker brought into being mighty Thunderbirds
with lightning in the blink of their eyes and wings of
cloud to carry life-giving rain.*

He hid giant monsters in the rivers. He made them
battle with the Thunderbirds in the springtime to swell
the rivers, flooding the land and filling the swamps, so
that everything with roots can drink.**

*Thunderbirds are careful with their power.
It is the young and wild ones who cause damage.
**When Underwater Monsters breathe in,
water spills over and floods the land.

When Earth Maker had finished all these things, he peopled the Earth with all kinds of beings. He shook the robe which he wore over his shoulders, and flocks of happy birds of every color flew out. They all understood him when he spoke, and in time he gave each one of them the right place to live.

Earth Maker spread his robe on the ground, and as he walked slowly, dragging it by one corner, hosts of animals of every kind ran out from underneath. They all understood him when he spoke, and in time he gave each one of them, too, the right place to live.

At first he put the Antelopes in the mountains, but they ran too fast and fell down among the rocks and hurt themselves. He saw that this was wrong and so he led them to the plains, where they could run fast, and there they still live happily.

In the beginning he told the Bighorn Sheep to live on the plains, but they liked best to jump among the rocks, and so he took them high into the mountains. They loved the cool air in summer, and that is where they still live.

While Earth Maker was walking around finishing everything, putting Grasshoppers here, Flies there, and Mosquitoes everywhere, he was thinking to himself: "These plains are immense. I will make four-leggeds who are strong and love the hottest sunshine as much as the coldest wind. They will be black and shaggy. The hills and plains will shake with the thunder of their young bulls fighting."

He spread his robe on the ground. Perhaps he was tired, lay down, and fell asleep, and while he slept multitudes and multitudes of Buffaloes came out from underneath the edge of his robe and spread out all over the plains, everywhere.

Earth Maker thought: "I will make two-legged beings and give them all that I have made. They will have hair only on the tops of their heads, and they will live together with the Buffaloes." And so it was that in his wisdom he scraped clay from Grandmother Turtle's back and worked it in his hands and shaped figures of Man and Woman. He laid them on a bed of sage leaves, covered them with cottonwood leaves, and left them to dry. Each morning he raised the leaves a little and peeped underneath.

On the fourth day Earth Maker lifted off the leaves and told the figures to get up, and he led them by their hands to the river to drink. He told them, "I am your Father and Grandfather, and the Earth is your Mother and Grandmother. I give both of you the joy and wonder of life, and of everything around you. I will always be close to you."

He said to Man, "I have made you strong against difficulties, and to be a help to Woman." To Woman he said, "I have given you kindness towards Man, your children, and all beings, and also strength to endure."

In time Earth Maker saw that People began to live in terrible dread of the Buffaloes. Buffaloes were larger then than they are now. Great herds of the huge, shaggy black beasts knocked down the tipis, and trampled the People to death, and even *ate* them. . . .*

Earth Maker was sad to see this, and so he taught Men to make spears and bows and arrows, and how to hunt. He gave Women fire to cook Buffalo meat and taught them how to make clothes from the skins.

Earth Maker told the People and the Buffaloes: ''This is how it will be now. You, Two-leggeds, will eat Buffaloes. But there will be great love between you, and you will live together on these plains until the end of the world.''

*The long hair on the chin of the Buffalo is the hair of the people he used to eat.

Earth Maker wondered how else he could help People: "They have to walk a long way looking for the Buffalo herds. It is hard for children and old people. I will give them a four-legged who will carry Men and Women on his back. They will feel proud to ride him! I will make him like the sky: gentle and sometimes fierce. He will have lightning in his legs and thunder in his hoofs; his mane and tail will be clouds, and when the People hunt the Buffaloes he will carry them and run like the wind right into the herds."

And so Earth Maker gave People herds of magnificent Horses of every color.

And then Earth Maker spoke to all the People: "I have promised always to stay close to you. I love all of you. Whenever you need my help on your path through life, talk to me! Sing! I am listening. Look for me on the hilltops and in the mountains. Hear me in the Wind and Water, the Crow and Coyote. I will come to you in your dreams and give you the wisdom of the Elk or Eagle, the Rock or Thunder. Think about all these, and they will teach you everything you want to know.

"Remember that only the Earth remains forever. Try hard always! Let all beings be happy!"

At the last, Earth Maker piled up high mountains at the place where the sun goes down, to hold back the waters from flooding the land and engulfing Grandmother Turtle.

He told Bull Buffalo, with his strong curved horns and powerful shoulders, to push against the mountains. Bull Buffalo is strong and he will live for a long time, but not forever! He grows older, and every year he loses one hair, and in each of the Four Ages* a leg breaks. When Bull Buffalo dies, the mountains will break apart and the waters will flood in once again . . .

*The Rock, the Bow, the Fire, and the Pipe Ages.

*The wise men have told us that Bull Buffalo is now weak and tired; he has only one leg left and he is almost without hair.*

. . . and then Earth Maker will make another world.